Happy Valentines Day
to Chet
from your Old Dog, Jane
February 14, 2000

Design and production by Heather M. McElwain.

Published by WILLOW CREEK PRESS, INC.
PO Box 147, Minocqua, WI 54548

For more information on Willow Creek Press titles,
call 1-800-850-9453.

Library of Congress Cataloging-in-Publication Data
  Smith, Steve.
    Just puppies / text by Steve Smith. -- Half pint ed.
       p.   cm
    ISBN 1-57223-219-6
    1. Puppies.   2. Puppies--Pictorial works.
  3. Photography of dogs.   I. Title.
  SF426.S62   1999
  636.7'07--dc21
                              98-52370
                              CIP

Printed in Canada.

PHOTO CREDITS

For Sarah Virginia

TABLE OF CONTENTS

Portraits

*The way we'd love
them to stay*

*P*ups – they're so irresistably cute that we can't help but brazenly pose them for ridiculous-
ly sentimental photos. When you think about it, these are the same mandates new par-
ents impose on human babies as soon as the kids are old enough to be dressed up and
masqueraded in equally preposterous poses. The difference? Puppies relish these sessions much
more than human babies do.

*S*o tiny, so fragile, so loveable. Nuzzle a puppy to your cheek, feel and smell its satiny coat, its unconstrained, fragile respirations, the distinctive aroma of puppy breath, the fleeting, unforgettable nuances of doggy youthfulness.

S o helpless, anxious, worried, apprehensive, defenseless. How can you not run to their slightest whimper, their least solicitous cry for help or attention? Huh, sucker? How can you not?

*I*t is universally assumed that all puppies are adorable and irresistable. "Universally assumed," of course, means that puppies understand this too. Observe the way they look at you: the pleading eyes, the innocent stares. You *know* what they're saying: *C'mon, couldn't ya just love me?*

*A*nd while it can be said that some pups
are so ugly they're cute . . .

. . . others are so butt ugly you just hope they'll outgrow it.

*B*ut big or little, black or brown, boy pup or girl pup, the common denominator is their time of innocence, wonder, and discovery and the entertainment value we get from watching them which passes so quickly. Let's face it: If you can't smile at a cute little puppy, you're actually a pretty hopeless creature yourself.

*A*ll puppies deserve a good home. The fact is, there are too many – cute and otherwise – for the homes available to them, and in some cases, the overpopulation is nearly epidemic. The only answer is spaying and neutering – in effect, resisting the nearly overpowering urge to bring more bundles of cuteness into the world unless there is a ready home waiting for each and every one.

The First 100 Days

Building the bonds

*T*he first day of life begins with mother and puppies equally exhausted by the ordeal and strain of birth. At first, the pups will be nothing more than whining, nearly immobile little slugs that eat and sleep and keep Mom hopping as she cleans up after them, in true motherly fashion. In a couple of weeks, the pups' eyes will open on to a new world. A few days after that, they will start their first, exploratory forays away from their mother (but not too far). The young dogs mature quickly, ready – according to canine behaviorists – to leave the litter behind and take their places in human families on the forty-ninth day of life. Until then, if you own the litter, God help you.

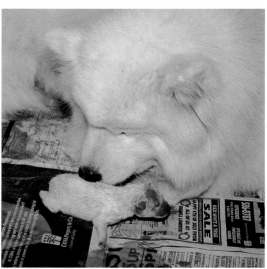

*T*he days pass in a warm, restful reverie of sucking and sleeping with Mom and littermates, comfy and secure. What will this little fellow or lady become? A guide dog? A search and rescue dog? A therapy dog? A hunting companion? A trusted family friend? Like us at birth, the future lies ahead. Unlike us, if the pup is a purebred, it has been genetically engineered through selective breeding for a specific role – to be anything from a cattle-herder to a police officer. But he or she can still be your buddy. No law against it.

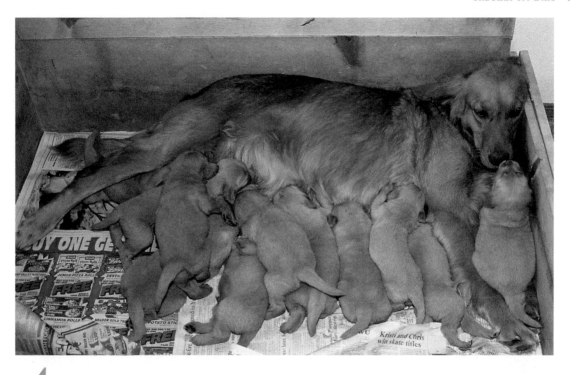

A newborn litter of pups are peas in a pod, at least at first. They care only about Mom and what she can give them – food, warmth, and shelter. Later, they'll start to explore their world, but for right now, it's good just to be very still.

*T*oo many puppies, or too few faucets? Seems like there's always one pup that gets edged out of the food line early and often, resulting in the well-known "runt." Of course, it's often the runt that ends up being the world-beater thanks to all that extra affection we lavish on it.

*T*olerance, defense of the litter, uncondi-
tional love – nature has built this devo-
tion into Mom at the sub-atomic level.
For seven weeks – from whelping to weaning –
it's what she does; it's *all* she does.

*T*here are several of life's decisions that should be pondered much more than they are: marriage, having children, picking out a puppy. Although each has far reaching, long-term repercussions, the truth is we usually spend more time ordering from a restaurant menu than we do deciding on a pooch. There are tests for dominance and submissiveness, tests for sociability, tests for willingness to please, and others we can give puppies, but no one in recorded history has ever used them to pick out a dog. That would be too logical. So, instead we simply pick the cutest one.

*T*he Night of a Thousand Howls – a puppy's first night, or two or three, is an unusal exercise in patience. Like human babies, they often get their days and nights turned around; unlike human babies, a new pup will miss mom and all those brothers and sisters – the puppy is alone for the very first time. You don't count, at least not yet.

*T*he first night, as any rookie owner will avow, is an exercise no one within earshot will ever forget, partly because everyone will be awake through the entire thing. The rationale here is as follows: *If you yowl loud enough and long enough, someone will miraculously appear. They will say something to you in a rough tone of voice, but since you can't understand them anyway, just wiggle and wag your tail and try to look pitiful. As soon as they leave the room, let 'em have it some more. Eventually, you will wear down The Opposition. This is how you get invited into somebody's bed the second night in your new home. And to stay there for the next fifteen years.*

*T*here are new rules, new commands in this new home. Who can blame the pup if, for a few days, he wonders about the wisdom of it all?

*T*he first salvo in the great conflict we call "training" is housebreaking. This absolutely *must* be accomplished as soon as possible. Pups are quick, and the urge to squat hits them with meteoric speed – and you have to be ready. The first few weeks are a series of accidents interrupted by brief periods of optimism in which you think Rufus has the going-outside thing licked. the unwritten rule for cleaning up after the pup is as follows: "The family member who first suggested getting a puppy will clean up after it." Kids, of course, are exempt from duty based on the fact that they'll either do a lousy job of it, or they won't do it at all.

The little puddles on the kitchen floor or – more likely thc living room carpet are easier to forgive than the brown surprises that you find where the pup has been off by himself in a secluded corner. It is essential that the little scofflaw be taken outside immediately after eating, and I mean immediately; first-time dog owners quickly find out that a puppy is a hollow tube through which you pour food and water.

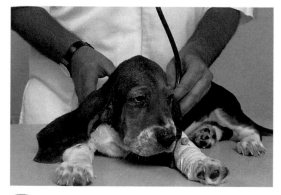

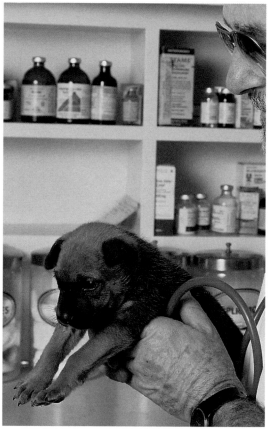

Of all the experiences your new family member has to assimilate, the one that never really seems to take is the value of proper veterinary care. Each pup is born with the genetically encoded information that anyone in a white laboratory coat exists to inflict pain and humiliation at regular, predictable intervals. They seem to view the experience the same way we would look at, say, a body-cavity search. Dogs that do not know their own names at age sixteen will learn, at the age of eleven weeks, to spell. Announce, "It's time to take Henry to the V-E-T," and watch Henry vanish like a snowflake in a campfire.

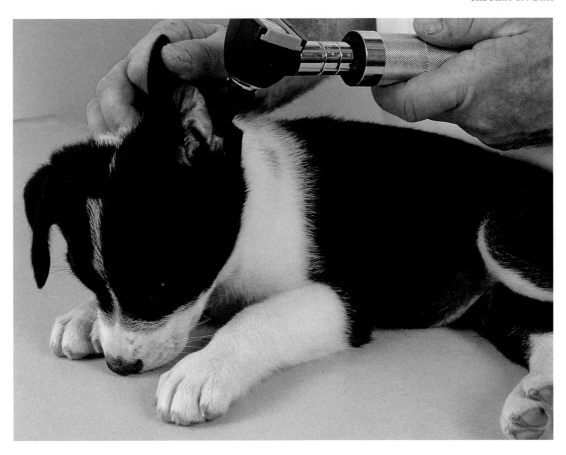

*T*he choice of just the right name is of paramount importance – some people go so far as to buy baby name books and leaf through them for inspiration. It must be a name that fits the dog's personality, of course, but it must be one that can be heard at a distance, because the chances are for most of the dog's life, you'll screech the name with all the stops tied down. "Malcolm," for example, doesn't carry nearly as well as "Jake" in the frosty, morning air as the mutt in question is leisurely opening the neighbor's garbage bags and you're on the front porch in your bathrobe. Unlike Americans, who eschew titles, the pup will have a title attached to its name, as in, "Jake You Knothead," or, "Jake You Furball," or, "Jake, you S.O.B.!"

The name is not, of course, a constant. It will be cannibalized – "Jake" will become "Jaker," or "The Jakemonster," or "Jock" or "Jocker" until none of you, including whatshisname, can remember where you started out.

If the name is important, it pales next to the choice of voice. This voice is used by all family members as they carry on two-way conversations with the puppy, and lasts throughout the dog's life. You speak to the dog; then, using the dog's voice, you answer back. Entire clumps of dialogue are carried on this way (although not when company is within earshot). After awhile, the dog comes to recognize the voice as being its own. Don't tell me you don't do it. We *all* do it.

Socialization – that's a fancy word for getting your pup to act well-mannered, the process by which he or she is turned from a feisty, brawling, contentious little yahoo into a model citizen. Apparently, the theory goes, the pup is socialized just by hanging out with us. It's supposed to work so that all those good, human traits we value so much rub off on Spot, and the dog becomes something other than a dog, which begs the question, "If what we wanted was something other than a dog, why did we get a dog in the first place?" And what good, human traits do we suggest he pick up and imitate – aerial bombardment and cheating on income taxes?

*T*he reason why pups must be socialized is, of course, that the puppies will live out their lives in human company and all its entanglements. They must, then, learn the concept of civilization, the act of being a good citizen in the company of humans and other dogs. The essential skill learned through socialization can be summed up as: *NO* – as in, *no* drinking from the toilet bowl; *no* chewing on the furniture; *no* lifting your leg on the potted palm in the foyer (or the table legs or the stairway banister or the Christmas tree or Uncle Hubert who is elderly and has a tendency to doze off); *no* barking out the dining room window at squirrels raiding the bird feeder; and *no* leg-humping the UPS driver. There are more such things, of course, but the pup learns them in due time and internalizes or discards them at his own choosing.

Between the "no's" and the "bad dog's" and the other imperatives of puppies learning good manners, though, there should be ample time for "good dog's" and for allowing puppies to be puppies. Remember to give them some of their own space, and to allow them to know your gentleness of spirit. Your rewards will be tenfold, as will be those of your puppy.

The Days Are Just Packed!

So much to do, so little time

*E*xcitement! So much to see and do! A kennel can't keep a good puppy down. Or in. Instead, it's a mere, momentary impediment to a litter of adventurers rushing out to embrace the day and all that new life has to offer.

*T*he first order of business is breakfast . . .

*B*reakfast can be a meals-on-wheels affair, lazy-susan, or a culinary event on fine china.

*H*ow much wonder can there
be? The world is the puppy's
oyster – an exciting universe
begging to be explored. Every new
sight, sound, scent, and texture is novel,
requiring individual cataloging in the
young doggy's encyclopedia of memo-
ries; each day invites experimentation,
analysis, and intrigue.

New seasons and sensations continue to expand a puppy's realm of experience. In summer, there's an introduction to the aquatic world, suspension in stuff usually reserved for drinking, and the infrequent chance to behold the enrapturing reflection of another puppy – one almost as beautiful as itself.

Come winter, it means reveling in a glittering landscape, lungs full of frosty, invigorating surprise, a chance to frolic in an endless playground of downy, crystalline white.

*A*nd no matter the activity, the time, or the place, there's a head long need-for-speed and always rejoicing in each new day, shrouded in the melodious innocence of youth, no barriers to stay the unbounded fervor of puppyhood.

*T*he young of all creatures endure physical and mental growing pains. Awkward, bumbling tykes that they are, puppies are no exception to that rule. Their clumsy intramural scrapping and stalking and pouncing on one another, besides being loads of fun, are actually calisthenics that cultivate dexterity and enhance motor skills. Having the opportunity to hit a moving target – a littermate, for instance – not only accelerates that development, it also teaches puppies certain social skills, such as how hard they can nip a sibling before it bites back.

*T*he family kitty is snoozing in the backyard, openly inviting the puppy to pester it. At least that's how the puppy perceives this apparent lack of feline vigilance. Attack! It's not serious, of course, just another form of roughhousing between friends. But the cat is thinking, *just wait till that joker dog lays down for a nap.*

*B*eing young, puppies can't figure it out. These other critters . . . what are they? Something to play with? Will they bite me? Inquisitive, yet timid, puppies aren't quite sure what to do with the menagerie of odd-looking creatures they encounter. Friends today, perhaps, but in a few weeks a puppy will come to understand that these beasts were created for a single purpose – high speed chases.

*S*ure the chicken knows. Soon enough, these little devils will be annoying the feathers off of her and the rest of her friends, making an otherwise tranquil barnyard a venue of anxiety and panic. With puppies around, that's the way it's got to be, the natural order. *But right now they look so darn cute,* the old hen thinks, *ya can't help but love 'em.*

*I*n the sporting breeds, the genes of hunting ancestry make themselves known even in the first weeks of a puppy's life. Something catches the pointer pup's eye and it reflexively freezes in an intense stance, the retriever pup feels an inexplicable urge to fetch a stick tossed in the pond. For now, at least, these young hunters haven't a clue why they do such things.

A puppy is a mouthful of needle-sharp teeth driven by four legs and a sense of curiosity. How else are they going to learn to unravel life's mysteries (and your shoelaces), to discern what's edible and what's not? Huh?

*T*ry this experiment – place on the floor in front of the puppy these items: a fuzzy doggy toy made in the shape of a mailman; a puppy teething ring laced with genuine, imitation beef flavoring; and your grandmother's photo album from the old neighborhood. See which one Fido pounces on. Uh-huh. Told you.

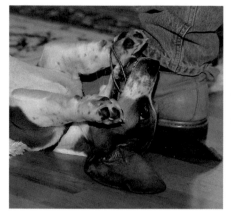

*E*ver gnawing, ever chewing, the unrelenting little savages shamelessly rend the garments of their benefactors. They not only bite the hands that feed them, they also steal and lose the gloves intended to keep those very hands warm.

*I*t's not their fault, of course. They don't know any better – and besides, those teeth *really itch*. And like a human baby, the pup's mouth is its primary tool of investigation through which it learns about its new world. Besides, they all eventually stop chewing. In about two years. The chewing, then, is just another part of the Age of Discovery – about life, what's going on, and where the pup fits in.

*A*ll this wrestling, exploring, making new friends, chewing – it's exhausting. Puppies don't choose to nap; it just sort of sneaks up on them.

*T*here's the pre-nap yawns – a series of portentous jaw-stretchers signaling the lights are about to go out in the puppy's head – and then there's that single, prodigious, postnap yawn, which is also a signal: You better take me out to the yard for a moment; I believe I have to . . .

Now just where did that puppy go? Oh, look, there he/she is, asleep on our new couch/chair/bed. How cute/adorable/darling/precious. He/she really shouldn't be sleeping there, but wouldn't it be cruel/unthinkable/stupid to wake him/her and make him/her go somewhere else while the house is so atypically/unusally/blessedly quiet?

*C*omfort also comes in various positions . . .